Personal Peaks

By Carol M. Schubeck

Published by The SuitCase Press
~~Post Office Box 6107~~
~~Orange, California 92863-6107~~
~~Tel: 800-796-1989 * 714-317-1989~~
Email: SuitCasePress@aol.com
Web page: www.suitcasepress.net

Copyright © 2002 Carol M. Schubeck

Written by Carol M. Schubeck, LCSW, CEAP, CAS
Illustrations by Rinna Clanuwat, BA

Library of Congress Cataloging-in-Publication Data

ISBN 0-9675567-1-6
LCCN 2001118778

Schubeck, Carol M.
Personal Peaks / written by Carol M. Schubeck;
illustration by Rinna Clanuwat. — 1st ed.
p. cm.
Library of Congress Control Number: 2001118778
ISBN: 0-9675567-1-6
SUMMARY:
Moving and Travel create personal opportunity for growth and change.
Developing your individual identity.
I. Moving, Personal Development
II. Schubeck, Carol Clanuwat, Rinna III. Title

Poetry; Health & Fitness; Nature, Body, Mind, & Spirit; Self-Actualization

To Yvonne,
May you
enjoy
each
Poem!

Carol

PERSONAL PEAKS

by Carol M. Schubeck

Illustrations by Rinna Clanuwat

The SuitCase Press
Orange, California

Adventurous Journeys

Foreword/Acknowledgments

Foreword/Acknowledgments

Each life enters the world on a journey of an unknown destiny. Parents, friends, family and the environment of the world shape each life. Many decisions and choices and experiences influence the journey. An African Proverb states, "It takes an entire community to educate a child." The poems collected in *"Personal Peaks"* represent lives embraced by many cultures.

I have experienced great pleasure creating a legacy of poems capturing "life on the go." May each reader be drawn to the wonders of the world known only through the eyes of the world. Our eyes are the windows of our souls. May your eyes experience the world as you travel the pages of *"Personal Peaks."*

My personal thanks to my parents who gave me the courage to move at age one, again at age nine, and begin my journey of seventeen moves. "Moving gave me the courage to do other scary things," states one teenager. I agree wholeheartedly.

Special gratitude is expressed to all the contributors of poems. Thanks for your tolerance of my urging, prodding, and insisting there was a poem inside your head.

Exceptional thanks to my family: Misty, Scott, Corina, Tom, Tibanni, and Sherry for listening endlessly to my stories of life in countries around the globe. Thanks to my editor, Jean Mather (English Professor at California State University) for your encouragement and professional skills, which have enhanced each of my publications.

Heartfelt gratitude to my friends worldwide, who have enlightened me with intriguing ideas, Eastern religious practices, a conscious commitment to the environment, and a devotion to our planet. Rinna Clanuwat's talent speaks volumes as her illustrations bring to life the stories, poems and testimonies of *"Personal Peaks."*

May you enjoy the living, moving and traveling experiences of each poem. Robert Browning captured the essence of "Personal Peaks" in the following quote:

> " *A man's reach should exceed his grasp*
> *or else what's heaven for?"*

To The Reader

As your browse the pages of "Personal Peaks" sit back and place your body and mind in readiness.
Readiness? What does this truly mean?
Allow yourself the time and pleasure of each poem and story.
Gently experience the joy of being with each experience.
May each poem and story open your mind and soul to being in the "now moment," away from the tension of life's obligations.

Helen Keller wrote, *"Life is either a daring adventure or nothing at all."*

Believe in your dreams and goals. Use your imagination to stretch into new ideas and new dimensions. Take the adventure risk that each author has embraced in "Personal Peaks." Create your own path.

TIMING

"Of all the knowledge, the wise and good seek most to know themselves."

William Shakespeare

I JUST CAN'T MOVE NOW

By Carol M. Schubeck

I AM THE President of the Ladies Guild
Chairman of PTA
Just made VP status of my corporate position
Fundraiser for the Charity Ball
Johnny is in the 8th grade
Sean - just potty trained
Mary is a senior in high school
Just wait, Just wait!

SUITCASE

By Carol M. Schubeck

Work, Pleasure, Sightseeing
70 inch, 40 inch, 22 inch wide
With rollers, carry on, oh my!

Does it fit, push and shove
Will this size be enough?
Oh buy another!

Here Comes The Van

By Carol M. Schubeck

Big wheels, smell of tape,
Boxes of all size, and many workers.
The truck size is awesome.
The workers are consistent in size and skill.
Supplies consume an entire room.
The blankets pad my precious pieces.
The crystal and china padded in place.
Boxes, boxes, boxes, stickers and numbers 1-3,000.
Oh, are they all necessary?
Definitely So!

WHEN IS THE RIGHT TIME TO MOVE?

By Carol M. Schubeck

It is never the right time to move
Moving happens when it happens
No planned schedule will do
No date is totally coordinated.
Each move unravels us more,
Unleashing wisdom and joy
Increasing our personal confidence and spiritual trust.

WHY MOVE?

By Carol M. Schubeck

MOVING ROLLS YOU INTO A NEW PLACE

MOVING PUSHES YOU INTO NEW SPACE

MOVING REVITALIZES YOUR ENERGY

MOVING IS LIVING.

WHY NOT MOVE?

By Misty M. Cushman

I've lived in this place for quite some time
"Time to Move," you say,
Maybe that will be fine…

Never knowing what adventure lies ahead
Around every corner…"May I please bring my bed?"

Maybe it won't be so bad, as long as you are there
Please hold my hand to show me you care.

Leaving

By David W. Timothy

Wine glasses filled
Family and Friends' laughter
Bon Voyage
Icing on a Cake

An airplane ticket
A backpack
My rite of passage
The Toughest Job I Ever Loved

ODE TO A MOVE

By Carol M. Schubeck

What will I find?
Who will be my friend?
Where will I live?
Can I shop?
Which beauty salon or barber shop?
Is it hot or cold, humid or dry?
Are there bugs or snakes or monkeys?
Maybe an elephant or gecko?
Who can I count on when I am alone?
Does sign language and pointing work everywhere?
Smiles, bows, gracious hellos
Food, Customs, Holidays unfold
Help me to find a new home where I can be me.

RISK

"We cannot discover new oceans unless we have courage to lose sight of the shore."

Anonymous

ON THE GO

By Carol M. Schubeck

TRAVEL, GO
BUSINESS MEETINGS, GO
THE SUITCASE AND I MUST GO

OH WORLDLY SIGHTS,
MY TRUSTY SUITCASE AND I WILL GO.
LOOK, SEE, TASTE, SMELL
GO, GO, GO
MEETINGS, DINING, SEEING, TASTING,
MY TRUSTY SUITCASE AND I WILL GO.

ASIA, EUROPE, AUSTRALIA, SO. AMERICA, HAWAII
MY SUITCASE AND I WILL GO.
FROM THE MOUNTAINS IN NEPAL TO THE BEACHES
OF AUSTRALIA
CAN I CARRY IT, CAN I BUY IT, CAN I CAPTURE THE
MEMORIES
WATERFALL, MOUNTAIN, BEACH, SAND AND ALL?

EXPERIENCE IT, FEEL IT, SEE IT ALL,
MY SUITCASE AND I WILL GO.

My Wanderlust…

By Fredrick Cole

Some feel the wanderlust to travel; others are content to stay put. For me, seeing other places is exciting, interesting, and even rewarding. Staying in one place makes things stagnate. Only those that are willing to travel can truly experience real wanderlust. The urge to travel has always intrigued and excited me. It stimulates my inner self.

This all started when I was a small boy. My family took vacations almost every year, and we moved from Wisconsin to California when I was seven. Traveling on old Highway 66 caravaning like a bunch of gypsies. We learned to bond together in those wondrous times. It was like being drawn somehow to another beautiful destination we could only imagine. We were just like all those immigrants before us; we were going to California for a better life. It was my father who took that big step, that challenge, with a wife and six boys he had no job, yet he had a dream that was unknown to us. This was the start of the urge to travel for me.

My three years of service in the in Army in Germany allowed me to travel around Western Europe. I loved it! I saw places that most people only read about or have never heard of or seen. I learned about different ways to travel. This enhanced my interest in traveling, and it gave me a sense of confidence.

After the service I returned to California and again moved around frequently. I pursued other passions of mine, the outdoors, wild things and of course, solitude. The urge to see different things is always on my mind, and I prefer to be in wild areas. It is my niche.

Traveling around the country has shown me contrasts between urban and rural areas. Population increases will limit the future wanderluster's ability to see wild things and areas as they once were. Because of the rapid growth in our country, time to enjoy what we have is limited.

A vocation in the outdoors gives those with wanderlust an amazing combination and opportunity. Seeing what our creator provided us is an awesome privilege. Protecting for future generations, our wildlife, resources, and habitats is a tremendous challenge, career, and experience. Eureka! I found my special job. So it's with me; I have one of the best jobs for the wanderlust, and it is being State Fish and Game Warden. Travel is a large part of this job. In the twenty-six years as a warden, I have traveled throughout California and the West Coast.

California is unique. It has a wide range of climate zones, habitats and wildlife. Future generations will not be as fortunate to experience what we have, because population increases will limit the wild beauty of it all. This will push the wanderlust in me to move on...

Many things to see are all around us in this world of ours, yet only those that put traveling a priority in their life will reach the level of the wanderlust. It takes a free spirit, a commitment, and a willingness to take a chance that it is all worth it. We have those challenges in life that tell us to go for it, but only the person who has the inner soul gripping willingness to travel can truly experience Wanderlust.

F E A R

By Carol M. Schubeck

What is this word that dooms our joy?
Fear conjures up dark, dreary, anxious thoughts.

Fear is your friend.
A temperature of emotions commanding attention;
A reduction of pace
An inner barometer stating more information is needed.

Fear brings doubt and caution
Fear can open your wisdom and learning experiences.
Fear as a friend bridges the gap of anxious thoughts
Emerging as tranquillity and energy.

Do you know fear as a friend or foe?

I'M MOVING AGAIN

By Matthew S. Neigh

I'm moving again...
Bags are packed like so many times before
Boxes cover my bedroom floor

I'm moving again...
Saying good-by to places and pets I hold so dear
Knowing memories of them will always be near

I'm moving again...
Wiping tears from my friend's eyes
These are the toughest good-byes

I'm moving again...
And though this chapter of my life may be done
I know so well that the next exciting one has just begun!

LEBANON TO CALIFORNIA

By Fred Hallak

Moving two blocks or 2000 miles
It is still not easy.
Not forgetting your friends or your country
Or the things you have known.

Enjoying the plants when I arrive
Watching how they grow
Knowing I will grow
Meeting new people and making friends
Smelling the ocean and riding my bike.

Travel

By Lois Kennedy

Too long the boredom of routine
I yearn for something else
Knowing:
Just around the corner adventure awaits
Excitement and fear,
New foods, sights, and smells
People of all colors and creeds
The expansion of my thoughts, beliefs, and limits
Thank God for travel !

Sunset on the bay
Fluttering wings
Come to winter in eucalyptus trees.

By Kathleen Dolores Day

OPENNESS

"We are all travelers in the wilderness of this world, and the best we can find in our travels is an honest friend."

Robert Louis Stevenson

Courage

By Carol M. Schubeck

Expand your world and your being
Like a sword straight and strong

Quiver as a feather
Cup as you grow
A line drive around the bases
You will score new growth.

Perceive, Persevere, and Grow
Bigger, Bolder, Braver as you go
What is your destiny? Where can you and I go?

ODE TO THE WONDERING OF LIVING FAR AWAY FROM HERE

Written By Jeanne Staivisky

Oh how I wonder and wonder and wonder

What is it like there?
What can I buy there?
What can I do there?
What can I wear there?

Oh how I wonder and wonder and wonder

Will I make new friends?
Will I like the food they eat?
Will I like the people I meet?
Will my friends remember me?

Oh how I wonder and wonder and wonder

As I apprehensively search the Internet
And learn about the promise of wonders
Yet to come in my new home far away from here.

TRANQUILITY

By Carol M. Schubeck

To know each other in unspoken words
Connecting at a level of divine being.

No words, No action

Simple awareness of a presence.
The same awareness a child experiences
Love, joy, spontaneity

There is but one universe of kindred souls.

RAJAN'S MOUNTAIN

By Rajan Karki

Trekking up the mountains
The Himalayan Mountains so high,
The mountains call to me
Speaking the truth.

On the mountain, I am free,
Free to be
Free to experience peace and solitude,
Clean air and wandering with the trees,
Walking in the forests of pine and fir.

On the mountain, I am curious and free.
Walking, climbing, listening, breathing thin air
I am climbing so high.
Rhinoceros, Elephants, Crocodiles, Monkeys, and Deer,
Goats, Jackals, Yaks possibly a glimpse of a Bengal Tiger or
Snow Leopard
I am a bird, a tiny swallow, free to fly, and oh, so high.

TREKKING TO THE TOP OF THE WORLD
By Carol M. Schubeck

RICE FIELDS, BACKPACKS, GENTLE SMILES ABOUND
SHERPAS, GUIDES, AND PORTERS,
STEP BY STEP, I SEE THE PATH
STEP BY STEP, SMELLING THE FRESH AIR
STEP BY STEP, BUTTERFLIES VISIT ME
WHERE AM I GOING?
TO THE TOP OF THE WORLD

HOW HIGH CAN I GO?
HOW HIGH CAN I REACH?
HOW HIGH CAN I BREATHE?
HOW HUMANLY HIGH CAN I GO?

MY BODY

By Carol M. Schubeck

Strong legs, Open heart

Judging not and being free

Time stands still for tender dreams

Time stands still for dramatic views

Inching along, I am new

I Dream

GROWTH

"Character cannot be developed in ease and quiet. Only through experiences of trial and suffering can the soul be strengthened, vision cleared, ambition inspired and success achieved."

Helen Keller

FREEDOM

By Carol M. Schubeck

Who is really free,
Is freedom only for the wealthy or young at heart,
Can freedom be for me?

How can the journey set me free
Can the scenery of each land
Enable me to be?

Where is the joy of this journey?
What is there to learn?
Grow as you grow, know as you know,
Experience the freedom coming from your heart.

FULL

By Carol M. Schubeck

MY HEAD IS FULL OF EXPERIENCES

MEMORIES GOING FULL SPEED

COMPLETING MY GAS TANK TO FULL, NOT HALF-EMPTY

LONGING FOR HOME

EXPERIENCING EACH STOP

THE JOURNEY CONTINUES

WHERE IS THE NEXT STOP?

EMPTINESS

By Carol M. Schubeck

Seeing the world
Traveling the world
Experiencing world pain
Seeing the pain.

People hope
People seek
People feel
People are real.

I can see
I can feel
I am real
Please guide me!

The Guide

By Catherine Markert

He shows us the way
We walk ahead
He passes us
He waits at dangerous places
He reaches out to us
He talks to us
He knows we can make it
We know we can make it
He points out the wonders
He answers our questions
He orders our food
He arranges our lodging
He quietly encourages
He shows us the way
He never doubts us
He smiles
He waits
He leads
He tells us stories
We walk
We listen
We see
We learn

TIME IN A WORLDVIEW

By Carol M. Schubeck

SHALL I BE LATE?
SHALL I ARRIVE AT THE APPOINTED TIME?
SHALL I DAWDLE?
SHALL I SPEED?
WHERE AM I FOCUSED
TIME IS OF THE ESSENCE

WHO WILL BE MY COMPANION
ON THIS JOURNEY OF TIME?
WHO WILL LEAD THE WAY?
MAY THE TRUTH BE MY GUIDE
TO KNOW AND EXPERIENCE EACH DAY.

TIME

By Carol M. Schubeck

TIME IS SO SLOW WHEN I AM NEW
TIME IS SO FAST WHEN I AM PRESENT
TIME IS THE SAME
TIME SPEAKS TO MY HEART TO BE IN THE PRESENT.

R A I N

By Carol M. Schubeck

Thunder rolls the sky
Jagged flashes of light brightening the earth
One inch or Two
Droplets are nourishing the land.

Water nourishes my soul
Drink from a cup drop by drop
Or
Nourish my soul in a river
Flowing into larger, bigger, and unknown.

Moving On

BEGINNINGS AND ENDINGS

"What we call the beginning is often the end and to make our end is to make a beginning. The end is where we start from."

T. S. Eliot

Where Does It Shine?

By Sarah J. Mirasola

The miracle of a full moon!
Dancing on the waters of Rimini Beach.
Rising over purple, desert hills.
Tossing of the cloudy seas of a windy Wisconsin winter night.
Spotlighting playful baboons in Zimbabwe
Creating a path across peaceful Clark's Lake
Enchanting an English garden with radiance.

Oh, the magic…..the mystery….the memories…

Detach and Grow

By Carol M. Schubeck

Material World says yes, I must have.
Material World says don't let go
Material World ego grows.

Being present allows me to nourish my growth.
Spiritual presence
Flowers growing, birds singing, mountains rising
Quieting the inner chatter.

Rising and reaching
Above and Beyond
Experience the unknown
Soar the crevasse, walk the edge
Detach and grow.

MOVING OUT AND MOVING IN

By Jean Mather

Moving out can be easy.
I moved out of six houses when I was young.
My husband and I moved out nine times in eleven years.
"This month marks 22 years here" rolls off my tongue.

Moving in has reduced me to tears.
Young and old have tried our domain.

First came our 14 year old niece, hormonal and wild.
She tried the house, the rules, and accepted our support.
But we discovered a geographical change didn't
improve her previous behavior.
A few months passed, not yet a year, we wished her
well bidding her adieu.
To the airport, and she moved out.

Our kids are packed, graduated, and on their way.
Alone at last, we empty nesters plan to play.

A telephone call, one tearful conversation,
And my mother-in-law arrived on a 747 for a 24/7 estate.

At 89, she's healthy, and needs her family.
To live until at least 100 is her probable fate.

Welcome is one of those funny words.
Welcome takes away: The Empty part of nesting.
Although the world of travel awaits our embrace,
We now realize empty nests are just for the birds!

Moving in and moving out.
Moving in impresses the heart more than moving out!

A New World
By Annette Olson

We don't need
to travel far
to experience
life
A sudden trip
across town
to the Heart Hospital
opens our eyes

To a new world where
small things
everyday things
old things

Things once relied upon
assumed
taken for granted
expected

Now seen
wondrous
infinitely beautiful
new again

We don't need
to travel far
to experience
joy

The Journey

By Ruth E. Van Reken

Cancer has always been
A word
A word for others
Never for me.

A word
To dread.
To speak of
In "whispers"

"Did you know she has Cancer?"

A word
To define.
"Cancer survivor."
"Cancer Patient."
"She died of cancer."

A word
To ignore.
"It can't happen to me."
"Women who breast feed don't get cancer."

But suddenly…

A word
Some might use to define
Me.
Yes,
ME.

Is that who
I will become?
Just
A word?

Another statistic?
Will Ruth be
Just
A cancer survivor?
A cancer patient?
Will she die of cancer?

I do not know
The outcome of
This word
I have suddenly
Acquired.

But surely there is
A difference
In whether
A word defines
My disease
Or if it defines
Me.

And so,
Dear Lord,
As I enter this
Valley of the Shadows-
May it be
Just that.

A shadow
But not me.
For while I live
In this Body-
A body which
Cancer can attack-
Sometimes destroy-
This body is not ultimately who
I am.

May this be
The time-
The time to learn more
Of this unseen reality regarding
Who I am and
Who You are.

May
A word
Ultimately take me to
The Word-
The One Who is
My Savior and
My God. Amen.

THREE GRACES REUNITED

By Sarah J. Mirasola & Carol M. Schubeck
Illustration by Annette Olson

Together again at the pool
Nine years have passed, but we are
still cool.

From Carroll College to Arizona and In
between:
Oh the experiences we have known
And the places we have seen.

Joy, Love, Sorrow, and Tears
Have all been a part of the years.

Some friendships will last many years.
Ours will last forever.

AUTHOR

Recognized as an expert on "moving with children," Carol M. Schubeck has worked as an Author, Speaker, Trainer, and Psychotherapist for the past 30 years. She has broad experience as a psychotherapist with healthcare organizations, military organizations, non-profit organizations and Fortune 50 and 500 Corporations. Carol began her professional career in Wisconsin working with children and families who frequently moved and continued her professional role with seventeen moves. Since she has lived and worked in Asia, Australia, Europe, and the United States, her expertise in moving and travel highlight her communications. Currently, a California resident, she frequently guest lecturers on college campuses and radio talk shows. Carol also provides consultations for international moves and employee assistance for Fortune 500 Corporations.

Carol is recognized and sought internationally as *" consultant of relocation of all ages."* She is often quoted as, "the resource expert relevant to relocation."

Ms. Schubeck's credentials include: Licensed Clinical Social Worker, Certified Employee Assistance Professional, Certified Addictions Specialist, Overseas Assessment Inventory Assessor, and Trauma Specialist.

Carol's first book, "Let's Move Together" for ages 4-12 has been widely received and is currently being read in 22 countries.

Carol is available for lecture series, consultation, or written communication at Tel: 1-714-317-1989.

Illustrator

Rinna Clanuwat is a Graphic Designer, Packaging Designer, and Production Designer for theater play. Rinna has illustrated 2 books in the United States and she is the author and illustrator of 2 children's books in Thailand. Rinna earned a Bachelor of Industrial Design degree at the Department of Industrial Design, Faculty of Architecture, Chulalongkorn University, Bangkok, Thailand. Please contact Rinna Clanuwat at *kwangjao@hotmail.com.*

The Suitcase Press
Orange, California
www.suitecasepress.net

Journey Notes

Journey Notes

Journey Notes